FAUVERIE

FAUVERIE

PASCALE PETIT

*For Lucy
with best wishes
Pascale Petit x*

SEREN

Seren is the book imprint of
Poetry Wales Press Ltd.
57 Nolton Street, Bridgend, Wales, CF31 3AE
www.serenbooks.com
facebook.com/SerenBooks
twitter@SerenBooks

The right of Pascale Petit to be identified as
the author of this work has been asserted in accordance
with the Copyright, Designs and Patents Act, 1988.

ISBN: 978-1-78172-168-1
e-book: 978-1-78172-169-8
Kindle: 978-1-78172-170-4

A CIP record for this title is available from the British Library.

The publisher acknowledges the financial assistance of the Welsh Books Council.

Book Cover Art: Dragana Nikolic
Author photograph: Tobias Hill
Back cover photograph:
NOAO/AURA/NSF – original image
modified for creative purposes.

Author website: www.pascalepetit.co.uk
                www.pascalepetit.blogspot.com

Printed in Bembo by 4edge Limited, UK

Contents

Arrival of the Electric Eel

Each time I open it I feel like a Matsés girl
handed a parcel at the end of her seclusion,
my face pierced by jaguar whiskers
to make me brave.
I know what's inside – that I must
unwrap the envelope of leaves
until all that's left
squirming in my hands
is an electric eel.
The positive head, the negative tail,
the rows of batteries under the skin,
the small, almost blind eyes.
The day turns murky again,
I'm wading through the bottom of my life
when my father's letter arrives. And keeps on arriving.
The charged fibres of paper
against my shaking fingers,
the thin electroplates of ink.
The messenger drags me up to the surface
to gulp air then flicks its anal fin.
Never before has a letter been so heavy,
growing to two metres in my room,
the address, the phone number, then the numbness –
I know you must be surprised, it says,
but I will die soon and want to make contact.

Black Jaguar at Twilight

He seems to have sucked
the whole Amazon
into his being, the storm-

clouds of rosettes
through a bronze dusk.
I've been there, sheltered

under the buttress
of a giant, felt
the air around me –

its muscles tense,
stalking me
as I stumbled

through dense fur,
my father's tongue
wet on my neck

as I fell into a gulch,
the blackout of his mouth.
And when I woke

I thought I heard
the jungle cough – this jungle,
the jaguar safe

behind bars. I lean over
and touch his cage – his glance
grazes me like an arrow.

Portrait of My Father as a Bird Fancier

The man with an aviary – the one
sparrows follow as he shuffles along,
helping him with caresses of their wings.
The one a nightingale serenades
just because he's in pain – that's
the father I choose, not the man
who thrusts red-hot prongs in their eyes
so their songs will carry for miles.
He is not the kind to tie their wings. No.
My father's nightingale will pine for him
when he dies. My Papa
with a warbler on each shoulder
and a linnet on his head, the loner
even crows chatter to. He does not
cut the nerves of their tongues
so they will sing sweeter.
When my father's bullfinch has a bad dream
only his voice can calm it.
The hoopoe warms itself on his stove.
It leaps in the air when he wakes
and rubs its breast against his face.
It can tell what mood he's in at a glance
and will raise its crest in alarm
if Papa struggles for breath.
My father's chaffinch can bring him
all the birdsong from the wood.
He does not glue its eyelids
shut so it will sing night and day.
He does not make canaries trill so loud
that the tiny branches of their lungs
burst. I am sure of this, though I am just
an ounce in the fist of his hand.

Kissing a Jaguar

That first meeting was like I'd had
Virola snuff blown up my nostrils.
Alone with my father
in a room he called 'la jungle'

bubbles of champagne
exploded like thunder, my head
split by lightning.
When I got back to my hotel I retched all night.

The next morning I floated along the pavements of Paris
and found myself in the zoo.
All paths lead to the Fauverie
and this is where I come, again and again,

to where Aramis has stars for a coat
and his mouth is a sky-gate
the jaguar shaman climbs through.
And I keep going back to that first meal,

to the girl who dined with the *tigre*
in his den, while the mariposas in his nightrobe
opened their wings
and flashed their eyes.

Through those obsidian mirrors
the god of all that is wild
whispers what I must do – when I hear him
I put on the keeper's green uniform.

My keys swing
as I wheel the trolley of carcasses
out of the service room
into the passage behind the night-cages

to where the beast paces.
He's been roaring all my life,
even in his grave he's pawing the soil
with impatient coughs.

I bring a plucked goose, a rump of horse
for the Master of Animals.
I'm behind your trough now, Father, about
to place my offerings like a yagua girl,

strong from the kill of memories. But first
let me pout my lips through the mesh,
my palm-spine whiskers brushing yours
as I plant a kiss on each cheek.

Sleeping Black Jaguar

1.

A solar eclipse – his fur
seems to veil light,
the smoulder

of black rosettes
a zoo of sub-atoms
I try to tame –

tritium, lepton, anti-proton.
They collide
as if smashed inside

a particle accelerator.
But it's just Aramis sleeping,
twitching himself back

to the jungle, where he leaps
into the pool of a spiral
galaxy, to catch a fish.

2.

Later, the keeper tells me
Aramis has had surgery
for swallowing

a hose-head
where his hank of beef
was lodged. But

what vet could take
a scalpel to this
dreaming universe?

What hand could shave
that pelt, to probe
the organs

of dark matter, untwist
time's intestines
and stitch

night's belly
together again, only
to return him to a cage?

Lungs (Father Speaks)

I need all my concentration
not to fall off the ledge
of this mountainous breath.
It's as if I have to swim
every river of my body
just to wake up in the morning.
There are parks that I pass
by ambulance every few months,
unable to tell if what's clogging the trees
is snow or cherry blossom.
But at night, in between sleep,
owls settle on them.
Their names carry me through the pain –
my menagerie of chouettes,
grand-ducs, harfang-des-neiges.
Then I send myself to the Jardin des Plantes,
onto the path of nocturnal raptors.
Once, I managed to stretch out my hand
and stroke a barn owl
before it melted like snow
and I woke back inside myself,
fingering the old wound.
Ignore the smell of half-eaten mice
in your Papa's untidy lair.
Come again soon. Even that draught
you bring from outside
is enough for me to live on.
There are secrets only a father can tell you –
how your heart is a creature
that must not be startled, and your lungs
its wings beating in your chest.

Sainte-Chapelle

Just as a master glassmaker must rest the iron blowpipe
against his cheek between blows, so as not to suck
the flame into his mouth when he draws breath,

so must you let the sun pierce your window
and rest against your face. It also is a furnace,
one of many in the sky's workshop,

yet the earth lets sunrays rest along its cheek,
drawing just what it needs to paint in light.
I tell you this after visiting La Sainte-Chapelle,

as you lie on your less painful lung, only
half-listening, concentrating on each inhalation.
But I persist, as if I could conjure the fifteen

fifty-foot-high stained-glass windows in your flat,
sand grain by sand grain, each grisaille detail
fused at impossible temperatures. I tell you

how cobalt can be added to raw glass to make blue,
copper for red and green, antimony for yellow.
How the panes are held in place

with lead cames and iron rods. How they have withstood
a revolution and eight centuries of storms.
It doesn't matter that the trefoils and medallions

illustrate the Bible and you are not a believer,
that there are fire-horses, a golden calf, plagues, wars.
The history of our species is up in that chapel.

As you lie there sleeping, the radiant colours
play over the altar of your skin
while the oxygen pump chugs its hymn.

Fridge

That second visit, you led me into
the kitchen, told me to sit next to you
on the low bench in front of the fridge,
its door open, the light shining on your face,
the hum like the frozen seconds
just before an accident or a longed-for kiss,
your skin flushed from the effort of breathing,
the tubes from your nostrils slack.
Behind us the oxygen concentrator exhaled
as if we were in the belly of a fish, the walls
of the kitchen pulsed near, then far, you smiling,
then a frown as you gulped for air.
We looked inside the lit-up cave
and our cheeks almost touched, as you pointed
at possible courses: venison in deer blood,
calf's liver in cream. Blanched asparagus
for hors d'oeuvre, or twelve Bourgogne snails.
For dessert, lemon sorbet, or the pièce de résistance:
a box of petits fours. I did not know what
they were, so in between bouts of purse-breathing
you explained they were miniature iced cakes.
And here I am popping another into my mouth,
while you, who have barely any appetite,
go through your sixth, then wash it down
with pink champagne. Six times
I came to your tiny flat as if to an altar,
you the father and I taking the sacrament,
tasting my heritage from the shelves of that fridge.

Bullet Ants

Imagine, my father says, *what it would be like*
        if you'd grown up with me. How quickly

I obey, entering the elders' hut where
        he's the master of ritual. He's plundered

the nests where girl-ants work, his hands
        deep in their chambers. He's strapped

each huntress into the wicker mat – my Dianas –
        their thoraxes tied, legs and antennae waving.

O hook-clawed ones, my Amazons,
        your jaws that can drag a hawk wasp

down the path, that carry a water drop
        to your queen without spilling it.

What Father does next is to dip the ant mat
        into a brew then blow cigar smoke over you.

I can hear every click of your armour,
        the communal buzz that soars to a shriek,

the rouse of pheromones like the crack of fire
        as he presses you against my growing breasts

and two hundred stingers stab in unison.
        Imagine, my father says. And I do.

Portrait of My Father as Saint-Julien le Pauvre

You are reading *Le Monde* in the René Viviani Square.
You have thistles in your hair, earth blood on your clothes.
It is a sunny March morning, still early,
before they crowd in – the fountain of talking stags,
the pigeon you strangled as a boy, almost fainting with pleasure.
There's a bear near you with a knife in its heart,
a woodcock with its feet chopped off,
a bull with a hatchet through its ribs.
Polecats, lynxes, foxes, wolves –
you spear them all and more appear.

You spear them all and more appear –
polecats, lynxes, foxes, wolves,
a bull with a hatchet through its ribs,
a woodcock with its feet chopped off,
there's a bear near you with a knife in its heart,
the pigeon you strangled as a boy, almost fainting with pleasure,
before they crowd in – the fountain of talking stags.
It is a sunny March morning, still early.
You have thistles in your hair, earth blood on your clothes.
You are reading *Le Monde* in the René Viviani Square.

Lungectomy

When the surgeon clamps back the flesh
and saws through your sternum

that's my chance to look,
to see your heart naked

before the scalpel makes its tearing sound
through your right lung, where it's

tar-black, colour of a secret night
I can touch without gloves.

Pâté de Foie Gras

I'm trying to distract her, my younger self,
the daughter eating a slice, her body
shivering. She thinks all that's wrong
is that the meal isn't hot,
but as she swallows, waves
chill her gut. She feels
as if a steel pipe
has been shoved down her throat
and a flood of grain pumped in.
She'll store them for later – these sensations –
she's my duckling preparing
for the great migration, her liver
gorged to ten times its weight
so she can survive the flight.
Father's wiping his chin now
and when she asks why Christmas lunch is cold
he says it's pâté de foie gras de canard,
part-cooked, a whole lobe.
That raw day
she sends her stronger self
up, as she did when she was a child,
to float just below the ceiling
and keep watch. I'm that guardian.
I've seen the duck farms of the Périgord,
that each memory has a cage –
so many of them – some with broken beaks,
torn throats, maggots in neck wounds,
one with her tongue lolling from her mouth,
all of them panting in their tiny coops
below the funnels,
their heads that back off when the man
clamps his hand over their eyes
and stuffs the gavage in.

Your Letter is a Przewalski Horse

You ask me what I saw at the zoo today
so I tell you that I watched the Przewalski mare
for a full hour, how she's named
after the Russian naturalist who first
sighted her kind in the wild, though
the herdsmen call them *takhi* meaning 'spirit'.
How they became ghosts of the Gobi, extinct
except in zoos. And then I think
of your letter, the way the sun shone on it
that stunned morning, a heavenly messenger
from my vanished father, asking me
to meet you before you die, its silver pelt
strange as the sighting of a sacred colt
in the Valley of the Horses – sandy, dun,
caramel in the folds that I stroke and stroke
as it nuzzles in my pocket. Your
address and phone number black
as an erect mane in a Lascaux painting.
My stowaway that you ask to see now
and I refuse, not telling you about the bitter-
sweet nosebag I'm managing to feed it.
Your one letter that I guard –
the last hope of your species.

The World's Smallest Deer

The good moments are rare as a tiny deer
I come across at the zoo
just when I am lost.

Only fifteen inches high, with a rust coat
of stiff hairs
and velvet horns,

the male is not yet a father.
All he wants to do is lick my hand
and rub his wet nose in my palm.

Soon, I'll find my way
to the Monkey House
or the Nile crocodile

but I linger as long as I can
with the endangered Pudu,
stroking him again and again.

Just as I'd stroke Papa if he let me,
when I spot the hairs on his arms
and decide they're harmless.

Self-Portrait with King Vultures

I stand in front of N'Golo and Margot
and remember that Christmas when Papa said
I have thought of you every day of my life.
I had just met my vanished father
but this couple was already here, probably
he was on his pole and she plucking at her rat
much as they are doing today.
By New Year's Eve I had snow in my hair
like ritual feathers, decided to shelter in the nursery
where I found a king vulture chick
and a keeper feeding her through a glove puppet
so she wouldn't bond with humans.
I still feel those newborn mice in my mouth.
They squeak when Papa feeds me scraps
I've coaxed out of him, my beak down his throat.
I digest everything – eyes, bones, tails –
but when I sleep they climb back up,
flakes of white fur stitch themselves together,
even though Papa's dead now and the Amazon
has lost most of its feathers. N'Golo
and Margot gaze past me at their rainforest –
although I know they were born in a zoo
I have to believe this. *I am the Vulture-Father,*
I eat death, N'Golo whispers, *I eat grief.*

Le Sang des Bêtes

for Tom de Freston

From the métro aérien I glimpsed our apartment –
the French windows flung to the night,
light blazing like slaughter.

That tumble into the past
had the impact of a bolt-gun.

Did my father hang there
like a horse, headfirst,
back legs strung from a beam?

Did my mother freeze at the door,
her whinny
shattering the lightbulb?

My carriage moves on, past the dangerous
work of the mind

as it sorts through memories –
those that must
and must not be remembered

except as flashes from the train-tracks
of history,

or only confronted in animal form.

My parents in their horseheads
as if dressed for a masque.

The knacker
can't return the foal's head to its neck
but he whistles as he cuts.

Grenelle Market I

At first I only notice
the polythene it's wrapped in.
Then the snout disc
fastened to a front trotter
by a rubber band.

My own nose sniffs
but the day is still
clean. I look harder
under the caul
that glazes the cheek

with a milky bloom,
see a long eyelid
closed against my gaze
and an ear, the flap
open, as if listening for Mother.

I want to mother
the neck folds, my eye
creeps downwards, over
the sign that says
'cochon de lait'

and the price. Beyond which
the leg seems intact.
I drag myself away
from the suckling pig
only to find

its under-half
also on display. I don't
look directly at the sawn-
through spine,
the coils of brain.

Grenelle Market II

The black eyes
of skinned rabbits
sawn at the waist

stare at their lower halves –
just opposite them
on the chilled tray.

Blackbird

When they locked me
in the cellar

and told me to count
slowly to a hundred,

each number
became a blackbird's feather

and all the darkness
sang

through the keyhole
of my yellow beak.

Cellar

She has been down there
with her father for fifty years.

I call her 'she'
because she is the cellar 'me'.

It is that night
with its two-paned window

at the top of the curving stairs;
she can just see it beyond his hair,

gleaming with a shred of curtain.
Her head is lined with numbered doors

and set with rat poison.
Her throat is a narrow corridor

with an earth floor.
Her tongue is a soiled mattress.

One night and its electric cables –
the frayed seconds tick.

And she focuses there,
sends me out and up,

gargling *run!*
in her recurring dream.

She is the silence.
I am the scream.

Grenelle Market III

After what seemed like a whole night in the cellar
I climbed up into the street.
The world was still there –
the cow hearts and oxtails, the goose eggs
and sweetbread. Mimosa bouquets
next to giant cheeses of earth's larder.
The farm hens still had their plumage,
the cocks their combs and talons.
The counters smelled of raw light,
of butchering and fiesta. And as coins
passed back and forth, my memory of the dark
vied with my appetite for colour, balanced
on those weighing scales just outside our door.

Lord of the Night

My father crept into the storeroom –
right up to my camp-bed.

He closed the door so gently
even the spider didn't hear.

He took out a handkerchief
and whispered that darkness

was wrapped up inside it,
passed it over my face.

Then he released a hummingbird.
The air vibrated,

I saw colours I had no name for
and a long needle-beak

that he pierced through my tongue
to keep me quiet.

Grenelle Market IV

Paris, to this six-year-old,
is a market tray
piled with lamb tongues –

it's only when she gets to Wales
that she can let herself
hear their bleats.

Blue-and-Gold Macaw Feather

Just a feather on the aviary floor –
I hold it to the light. Sapphire
one side of the shaft, lapis

on the other, like earth's arc
as it tilts into space.

And the underside, sulphur
as a field of rape, is a palette
where cadmiums roil.

I balance the fallen blade
between thumb and forefinger.

I could paint a world
with this brush, these hues.

Is this how God felt as He drew
His colours across the void?

North China Leopard (Tao)

His eyes are snow-globes. Inside
are galaxies tipped orange, then green,

his cinquefoils the pug-marks
of almost extinct stars, printed

on a gold velvet universe.
He paces and turns, his flank

falls and rises
with black holes, pulsars,

a host of them, and the white
under-belly's a wrestle

of light-year-long blizzards,
space where time reverses

and stalls, springs back, licked
by the tongue of stellar winds.

My Father's Wardrobe

after Peter Redgrove

In the late afternoon he begins his toilette –
he has limestone pyjamas threaded with fossils,
a nightshirt of catacombs through which his dreams drip.
He has a dressing gown woven with petrol fumes, between
    its folds
echo car-horns and the murmur of tourists.
He tries on the long rail of awakening suits.
He dresses from the quarries that built Paris.
He wears a cathedral cloak with chimera eyes.
His raincoat is stuccoed with spouting gargoyles.
He has trousers that are stained-glass windows,
casting shadows like candied fruit as he walks.
His cravat is a knotted métro train,
one tie is an escalator, another a fountain
with Saint-Michel fighting Satan.
A carousel turns silently between his knees
and in it a boy is singing on a lacquered foal.
He has a shirt of hotel fronts
and a waistcoat of bridges under which bateaux mouches glide.
He emerges from the trapdoors of nightclubs
in a wedding suit of pavements that steam in the sun
and in it he marries the dawn.
He has a jacket made of wind-blown newspapers
and a cocktail suit of cigarette smoke
with balconies for pockets. Sometimes
he wears a suit of ash that scatters when he moves.

Notre-Dame Father Speaks

Under the Seine I burrow,
through the medieval cellars of Paris,
from the rue de la Huchette to Notre-Dame.
Swimmer of sewers,
rat-father of jazz caverns and oubliettes,
haunter of nightclubs and dungeon vaults,
trapdoor and manhole opener,
dancer of the catacombs.
I am the father who searches beneath the water
and above the air, flying father,
ascender of four hundred steps
to the North and South Towers.
Father of the Chimera Gallery,
my names are Howler, Gnawer, Goat.
Eroded father, I lightning out.
I am the angel of the great nave roof
blowing my bugle.
Throat father, I gurgle forth.
I am a dove perched on a demon,
my beak always open.
My heart is a rose window.
Quarry father, stroller of the necropolis,
caretaker of the quai Saint-Michel,
resident of Les Argonautes hotel,
my gargoyle eyes see the insides of things.
I am the gypsum and limestone father,
my left foot is a crypt
and my right a foundling hospital.
Doctor and priest father,
who heals as he wounds,
I go in and out of the realm of death
to where the sicknesses crouch.

Notre-Dame Father Speaks (Palm Sunday)

You summon me, with my uni-horn
on my chimera brow. Nine times
I knock and the bolts draw back.
See how the air hallows me
as I slip in with the rabble,
not on a donkey but a goat –
cloven-hoofed father, devil-saint.
Batterer of doors,
parter of virgins' thighs.
I cross the threshold
dripping Seine and sewers,
grave-mud on my face,
my tongue a lightning fork.
Under the Last Judgement I pass,
Lucifer, Gabriel, say – *Enter!*
They weigh my soul
over the procession of the damned.
Beneath the twenty-eight kings of Judah
and the great organ I trot –
Pan of the forest pipes
who makes the dead rise
in a whirlwind of incense and hail.
Father of the west rose window,
with wings of molten glass rays,
each feather an illuminated book,
my halo whirling with the zodiac
as the lintel shakes,
thirteen crescendos of colour
vibrating in streaming air.
Penetrator of the Holy of Holies.
The congregation loves me,
they roar as the organ booms.
Wine says, bread says – *Enter!*
Sunlight smokes through the central portal
as I ride up to the altar,
into the stained-glass womb
of your cathedral mother.

My Mother's Salmon Skin Nightdress

With my pot of fish bladder glue
and my fishbone needle, my fish thread,
I am sewing my mother's nightie.
All my childhood I sew, mending it until bedtime
and each morning it's in tatters.
I mutter like a Siberian seamstress
as I scrape and soften new skins.
I study clouds to paint on her hem.
I came from the waters of her tummy to do this,
but each night she lies like a gutted fish
for Father the fishmonger. He strokes her
as if she's a salmon on a bed of ice
that should be dead but is still twitching.

Lapin à la Moutarde

You ask me to tell you what feeding time was like
so I start by saying how keyed up the big cats were, ready
to pounce on whatever the keepers thrust into their chutes –
the snow leopard shaking his turkey, the clouded leopards
tearing into white chickens. You nod and say
there is something you must tell me but not yet,
we have a meal to share, and once
you've told me your news everything will be spoilt.
The home help has prepared oysters, followed by
lapin à la moutarde, for dessert there's tarte tatin.
What happened next was that the snow leopard
bolted his turkey but seemed confused
with his rabbit, pacing back and forth
with it dangling from his jaws, blood trickling
down the long white ears. I show you the video
I took of his performance, my iPhone between us
as he yoyos from one side to the other. But I haven't
got this right because I filmed this twelve years
after your death, Papa, yet you are still chewing the last
    mouthful.
You lift the serviette to your lips and wipe them,
glancing at the clock above my head
as I replay the echoey voices inside the Fauverie,
one little girl crying *oh le pauvre lapin!*
It's closing time and as the guard ushers me out
the lights are suddenly switched off.
I'm biting into my apple tart as you announce
You no longer have a mother.
There's the story to work out of how you know –
the phone call from my brother when he couldn't reach me
    at home
and had a hunch I'd be here, my secret three days alone
in Paris before I revealed my arrival.

There's a reel in my head of a leopard
who doesn't know what to do with the gift of a rabbit.
Every now and again he interrupts his circuit
and darts his face forward, startled,
then he's back into the loop, perhaps
needing to bury his bunny for later or
take it somewhere where no one can watch him eat.

Squirrel Monkey

Because today every breath is a struggle
    I show you a photo of Baker
        the first monkey to survive in space.

She's in a capsule no bigger than a thermos.
    She wears a tiny helmet and space suit,
        a respiration meter fixed to her nose.

All we can see is her face, eyes looking up,
    mouth slightly open, her tail pinned
        beside her head. Her companion Able,

the rhesus monkey, is in a separate cubicle.
    She is alone. Imagine, I say, that you're
        strapped into the nose cone of a missile

shot into space. See the flash as you defy
    Earth's gravity and enter weightlessness.
        Your breathing quietens

as if you've risen free of your bed
    and the gifts of life float around you.
        You're concentrating on the rocket

and its little explorer, the trust
    that she'll re-enter our atmosphere.
        What does she think is happening?

As soon as Earth vanishes it reappears,
    the whole blue-and-green jewel,
        clouds parted like the moment

of re-entry to this room – an ocean of air
    hurtling towards you, blue sheets on fire.
        Now Baker is lighting up the sea

off Antigua, as she zooms down,
    bobs, then is retrieved. You smile
        as I describe the opening of her bio-pack,

how she scampers out and chews peanuts.
    You want to know everything – the press conference,
        how the ship's captain held her like a doll,

how Able died soon after, but not
    Baker. She lived twenty-five more years
        and even now, children place bananas on her grave.

Lion Man

All my life I have dug
with my hand hoe in the half-light
to piece you together –
half beast half father

with the head of a cave lion, legs
of a man. Right foot missing,
the left raised on tip-toe
about to dance. Dad-idol

with the dots and scars
of a trance. Pricked ears, flared nose,
whirler on the altar of time.
Moon yellow bone,

biter through rock-veils,
starer into frost-flames of the Ice Age.
Once, you were carved from the curve
of a mammoth's tusk,

from its nerve canal;
the pulp cavity became your spine,
calcium crystals
polished with spit and leather.

Still young
at forty millennia,
I turn you over in my hands –
twelve inches long like a newborn.

How to Hand-Feed Sparrows
(Instructions to My Father)

Stand at the box privet
just in front of Notre-Dame,
hold your arm high, your hand out flat,
the fingers bent back
so your palm is generous. Let
the sun burn the top of your head
as if it's a candle, a whole day
for it to ignite. And when
a sparrow lands, keep stock-still,
even though the flame is lit
and your scalp is melting.
You've laid your feast across your lifeline –
a galaxy of mixed seeds from the bird market
and she has chosen one of the elliptical grains;
it glows in her buff and saffron beak.
Rilke is just a shade
but you know he's there when she
takes off, then returns with friends
who hover and join in.
You can feel the draught from their wings
like a blessing across your cheeks
and the poet's words have tiny claws
that have gripped your skin.
If the crowd could vanish, in the end
even a seraph would come down and feed.
From your post on the low concrete wall
you can just see the stone angel
high on the western gable of the nave.
Keep your hand steady, support it with
your other arm, until your flesh is stiff as wax
while messengers of darkness and fire
fly down to taste your offering.
They are hungry, and you
have only one hour left of that wick
in the centre of your being.
Let it burn down to the soles of your feet.

A Tray of Frozen Songbirds

For our last meal together
my father takes out of the freezer
a tray of frozen songbirds.
He's saved them up, these delicacies
with ice crystals in their beaks,
wings stuck to ribcages.
There are skylarks, blackbirds, doves.
He tells me how some were plucked
while still alive,
about the mist net at dawn,
how one nightingale was thrust
into a sack of discarded heads
and cried, then the poacher licked
the sticky lime from its plumes
tenderly, before slitting its throat.
He pours champagne as if it's
the river of life.
We eat like two drunks
woken from dreams of flying,
me on his lap, singing the song
I've just learnt at school – *Alouette,*
gentille alouette, alouette, je te plumerai.

Hand

When I see your hand on the bedside table,
it's like swimming into a great cave
and in the beam of my headlamp finding
a thirty-thousand-year-old handprint.

You tell me you've lived near Marseilles,
over the calanques, and I imagine you
pacing in your cliff-top home, while below,
the Ice Age paintings wait in vaulted karst.

I think how these tobacco-stained walls,
after much staring, must flicker,
that when the pain in your chest
becomes ice-hot, you see dots explode

like sparks from the first fire.
I think of the harm a hand can do,
of what yours has done, how large
it was to a child, a red mist humming

over my nightlight, how white it is now
as you close your eyes and focus on breathing.
This old hand warm as limestone
that now places its palm over mine,

that the beasts gather round as if it might free them.
They slip from the shadows of your room –
the giant deer, the aurochs, even the bison
whose hind legs have been buried in rock.

Rue du Puits-qui-Parle

Rat-hole, oubliette, well-that-talks –
he's walled up like an anchorite.
There is no door now he's confined
to his bed. The plastic tube
that feeds him oxygen is his chain.
He discovers the silence within silence
like a well within a well –
and all his days are dry.
But some mornings, when a ray
pierces his window and dances
on the brown wall, he hears
the silence of still water
and the silence-after-rain.
He remembers rivers,
their surface striped as tigers –
golds and blacks ready to pounce
when night's claws grip his chest.
And there's a silence that hangs
like a sluice over the rim of his throat,
breath elusive as a diver's. My father
lying at the bottom of his cistern
like a glint of dried-up water, his back
arching from the ache in his lungs,
the weight of memories upon him.
He breathes in and the water strangles,
he breathes out fog.
Rats gnaw his sawn-through ribs.
The concentric walls rear towards
the light of his daughter's face
floating in the whirlpool's eye.
Long after she leaves, his voice circles
the Street of the Speaking Well, echoing
after her, down the cobbled alleys of Paris.

My Father's Mirror

My father's mirror went walking
through the streets of Paris

as if he had cut himself shaving that morning
and had gone back to bed, while his skin

floated up like a silver shadow then
slipped down the stairs.

He was a knife covered with solar blood,
a god of light and wind. Over his eyes

passed pedestrians, plane trees,
and he swallowed them.

He was a masterpiece, the jaguar
in the mirror that smokes.

He lit a cigarette, the lighter
brought forth apparitions.

Crossing the boulevard he reflected a car
so that it travelled backwards.

He was a glass map reading itself,
a small boy on his first adventure,

shivering with excitement,
the web of his city frosting his cheeks.

The sun carried him as far as the bridge
then he lay down and became a puddle.

The snow, when it fell, was gentle,
the flakes gathering

like a sheet drawn over his face.

Ortolan

When the doctor says it's just a matter of weeks,
my father arranges to have a chef brought in
with an ortolan still singing in its cage.
It's been blinded for a month, fattened on maize.
Father watches while Armagnac is poured in a bowl
and the bird plunged in and drowned. He thinks
that death will be like this: a singing in the dark
then the pop of a few last bubbles, while the
olive-gold feathers of his body are plucked,
his feet snapped off. Eight minutes he waits
while the bunting roasts, then it's rushed sizzling
to his lips, a white napkin draped over his head
to envelop him in vapours – the whole singer
in his mouth, every hot note. The crispy fat melts,
the bones are crunchy as hazelnuts. When
the bitter organs burst on his tongue in a bouquet
of ambrosia he can taste his entire life – heather
from the Kabylie mountains, Marseille's salt air,
lavender from Provence – he's flying through
high clouds to his nesting ground. Five years
he's been confined to this small room, grown thinner
despite the oxygen-rich tubes, his lungs
burning around the mute songbird of his heart.

Philippe-Auguste's Wall, Rue Clovis

The morning before he died, I like to think my father
yearned for one more glimpse of his wall.
That by late afternoon he might have been strong enough
to open his window and eavesdrop on the arguments of ants
as they hurried home across the bleached rampart.
That their quarrels kept him awake to catch the high-pitched
squeals of a stag beetle, and this took him back
to when he lived two doors down from Django, how
with the help of oxygen he managed to hum a few bars
of 'Oiseaux des Iles'. So, let's keep that window open,
his gown tied, the scarf warm around his neck, while he waits
for the shutter-click of a bat's flight. There's one hour left
to savour the rustle of a spider re-weaving her web –
no flies yet trussed on moonlight's net.

Portrait of My Father
as a North China Leopard

Up he springs from his sickbed, this father
who makes for the open

like an old leopard climbing the snows
of the Kunlun Mountains,

even if he risks an altitude
that could freeze him to a carcass of stars.

He staggers to the corner of rue du
Cardinal Lemoine, to the slope

with the sweep of Paris, his face
shining with the ferocity of his life,

his nightrobe behind him
like a pelt almost cast off,

heavy as a winter garden. He looks
down, across the Seine, over

to the right bank, to feast on the white
buildings and their coming lights.

Above them his quarry:
the hare of the moon and thin air.

No sound now that whiskers of rime
grace his cheeks, teeth bared like icicles.

My Father's City

All of Paris is quiet, while the oxygen machine
struggles to fill your lungs.

The gargoyles' cheeks flush
from the strain of breathing for you.

The clouds are still – they won't
steal one minute from this morning.

Around the Périphérique, cars
switch off their engines. Plumes of vapour

rise from the streets where you lived –
rue de la Huchette, quai Saint-Michel.

Sparrows have nested in your doorframe,
it's so long since it was opened

and I have come to give you a bed-bath,
to shut the flowers in your skin.

The Jardin des Plantes locks its enclosures
as I dry the garden of your chest.

The winged ghouls of Notre-Dame crouch
on your shoulders as you sleep;

they have guarded the scar between your ribs
the last years of your confinement.

Their stone eyes stare at me
as I shake your arm. And when

car horns and sirens fail to wake you
and the doctor comes to switch off your oxygen,

I see you stretched on your narrow bed
like an etiolated city, O my father, all your gates closed.

Harpy Eagle Father

When I think of my father in the furnace –
the gas jets aimed at his chest,
fire-wings budding from his shoulders
and his mouth opening with its lit interior,
his tongue delicate as an icicle –

I want to be a harpy eagle mother,
feed dainties into his beak, its red
gape wide open to the Amazon.
I want to guard my precious snowflake
unsteady on his talons in the hot nest.

I want to guide my chick as he inches onto a branch
and shakes the blizzards of his wizard-wings.
Oh take your time, I want to say,
before the fledge. Perch here to watch
the howler monkeys of this forest.

Wait before you grow coverts
grey as ash, your primaries lifting
in violet air. Let the combustion chambers
of your under-wings pulse
with maelstroms of white down.

May the double haloes of your body
lift slowly and your head sprout
its adult harpy crest. Before
you're off, up and through
the trees, trailing a smoky wake.

Lion

The day I cremated my father
I let my feet, which had been
pacing for three days and nights,
drag me into the cat-house, to where
the lion threw himself against his bars
demanding more horseflesh from the keeper.
Then he collapsed onto the straw
until someone roared back at him
and he leapt up to paw at the crowd.
I didn't think it was decent to stay there
the day of my father's funeral,
my hand still smarting from when
I'd touched him in the coffin,
that bruise-mark on his cheek
like raw meat. My old friends the pumas
chewed quietly on their bones
while the lion rose from the floor
and opened his jaws wide as Notre-Dame –
his breath like incense, his tongue a red nave
leading me through the fire of his mane.

Resurrection

I woke with the Paris streets tangled in my arms,
cobblestones bursting from my breasts.
I sprang up and dressed like an excited city
going for a walk. The Boul' Mich', yes

that street that bears your name, Father,
had clouds floating down it,
the banks of the Seine freshened
by a sudden draft of eagle air.

There are days when a daughter can pluck
her father's city out of the drains
and hold it up for the sun's inspection.
Domes, terraces, pleasure-boats, dripping from her

and the river up-ended in the pre-dawn light.
You, raised from the dead and me wide awake –
day's daughter – strong enough to upturn a capital,
to shake time to its roots.

And if you came to the door dressed
in the black suit of night
with stars whirling on your sleeves,
or in the white suit of day, with a sky-blue shirt,

what would I say to the humming dark
or the shouting light, the weave
of intersecting streets, traffic-thrum?
Would I let you into my house

in your coat woven with car lights,
your mouth yawning like a métro entrance?
If you came with a cathedral in your arms
would I welcome Sacré-Coeur into my kitchen?

Your Dressing Gown is a River

You are evasive as the Seine –
it's like there's a river in the room,
a silk scarf pulled from mud, your
khaki dressing gown a paisley motif
of copper and chrome lights,
a sleeve that gestures like the Bièvre
only to vanish underground.
Nights, you rear over me,
your face veiled by cloud
and I am six again, about to be
lifted in those drowning arms.
Then the sky tips and I'm
back on the quayside, legs
dangled over the edge, palms
pressed into stone. However hard
I stare at your surface I can't see in.
I'm a diver doing a fingertip
search along the silt of your bed
for evidence that you existed,
who finds your rusty hunting rifle,
a flake of skin lodged in the trigger.
I bury my face in the weave of currents
that still smell of you. My father,
who moved from place to place,
adopting foreign names,
who even in your grave
must be changing shape, your
body contours forming loops
that alter their course, dissolve, reform.

Effigy

I sat in my hut until you were ready –
father of earth and hemp, cobweb hair.

It was I who built the platform where your corpse rotted.
I waited fifteen years
until your skull was clean

before I pressed clay over your face
and painted it with tongo dye.

Because you would not say sorry
I placed your effigy in the men's house.

I braved the slit entrance.

I passed the poles mounted with flying foxes,
danced with croton leaves.

I watched the spirit puppets,
stuck the spear into the pig's heart.

No woman is allowed to do this.

Boar tusks gore to the truth,
looped around your cane arms.

A pig's jawbone is honest,

kauri resin doesn't lie.
Plant fibres don't avoid words.

Your bark belt and treefern torso
bear your penis-sheath proudly

here, in the Musée du quai Branly,
where you stand in a glass case.

This man is my father,
he speaks with the tenderness of flowers.

Clouded Leopard

It was raining when I saw
the clouded leopard, as he leapt
from branch to branch

as if from cloud to cloud,
his pads silent as raindrops
on the cage litter. I peered up

at the freedom above me
and thought I saw his ghost
descend a shaft of light

head-first, two long storm bands
balanced along his back.
His belly was a surprise downpour

and his paws spotted like showers.
Rainmaker, close cousin
of the sabre tooth,

extinct shadow that haunts him –
you will slip away unobserved
and there will be no others

of your kind. Your departure
will leave my earth parched.

Black Jaguar with Quai Saint-Bernard

Behind the Fauverie a crawl of quayside traffic
while Aramis roars for his food, the air
turbulent as he opens his jaws in a huge
yawn. If I hold my breath, half-close my eyes
and listen hard – there at the tongue's root,
in the voicebox of night, I might hear
the almost-vanished. He's summoning his prey,
this lord of thunderbolts, calling to ghosts
of the Lost World, with this evening chant
to scarlet macaw, tapir, golden lion tamarin.
Until everything goes slow and the rush-hour
queue of scale-to-scale cars is one giant caiman
basking on the bank. The jaguar's all
swimming stealth now – no sound – a stalker
camouflaged by floating hyacinths, senses
tuned only to the reptile of the road. Then, with
one bound, spray scatters like glass, as Aramis
lands on the brute's back and bites its neck.

Black Jaguar with Goat

He lies on his podium like a god,
commanding
constellations of eyes.

Yaguará – meaning
he-who-kills-
with-one-bound, who knows

how to bite the brain
clean.
Aramis, zoo-born, may not do this,

his caretaker says.
If a goat
were released in his paddock

she might run to the mesh
while he tore her apart
alive.

What is innocence?
He is devouring his meal as trained.
What is worse –

to be the too-real prey
or the predator
without instinct?

When I walked into your room Father,
I asked you to call me 'kid'
as if it were natural.

Every day I begged to be fathered.
I don't know when you
became the goat,

the blood draining from your face
as I became jaguar,
black roses staining

the umber of my pelt.
I don't know when you first
smelled the world

steaming from my mouth,
or how you managed to die
before the fires of your eyes

recognised their kin.
What is guilt?
You shrunk to a skeletal shriek.

We were all hungry —
the jaguar-goat,
the horned moon

staring through the window,
even the atrium of pent muscles
that is a city's dome.

We gorged but kept eating.
We died but kept living.
God watched us from his throne.

Caracal

Fawn-rust coat, no markings,
like the sandy loam I gathered
from your unmarked grave, Papa.

What happens to a body after fourteen years?
The keeper throws a steak
into the air and Black Ears

jumps ten feet to catch it –
it's like a desert doing a somersault.
If I am your keeper,

the temporary owner of this plot,
let me tempt your soul
with a meal, throw it higher

than the horse chestnuts,
into the clear blue air that quivers
with the cries of a goshawk.

North China Leopard (Leila)

After visiting your grave, Father, I go
straight to the Fauverie.

What I have to tell you about
is the fury

as Leila the North China leopard
dares the keeper to push her feast

into the chute and roll it round to her
without losing fingers.

I want the white rabbit of appetite,

to tear off the fur and spit it out
then gobble its heart.

I want all my Christmases in that turkey
she'll drag to her den.

She's clawing at the mesh
so fast it's like she knows

there are few left of her kind –
she's biting the bars of life.

Black Jaguar at Twilight

All day I waited for him to appear.
Now – everything is arrival. The minutes
cascade into a dust-slicked pool.

The coming night glows with eyeshine,
a velour tapestry of mygale eyes,
this emerald tattoo of fireflies

Aramis has brought on his coat.
His paws are talus slopes of wreathed plateaus,
his gaze their severe summits.

The trick is to stare through my reflection,
to squeeze through the grains of glass,
even slip time's membrane.

The self that approaches him must shuck
its human skin, wear a veil of fiery rain.

The Horsehead Fiddle
(Mongolian Myth)

I wish I could mourn you, Father, the way
the sky-rider mourned his wild horse
after its wings were cut off.

I'd carve you as a horsehead fiddle,
whittle your bones for the neck,
take hairs from your tail for the strings,

then stretch your hide over the soundbox
and where your head would rear from the scroll
I'd give you such fine ears,

turn them until you are taut.
Back and forth my bow would bend
as we galloped at star-speed

across the steppes, winds hoarse
but pitch-perfect, meadows
where you'd graze on the blades

of song, gulp pure springs
so you could throat-sing, not
that grating wheeze of smoke-black lungs

but deep belly-breaths.
And as my fingers drew your neighs
from the depths of my instrument,

how your hooves would fly, leaping over Orion
to race the Horsehead Nebula –
you'd lift me into the sea of grief.

Emmanuel

In the last days, after all he said
and didn't say, his iron tongue
resting in the open bell of his mouth,
the belfry of his face asleep,
I climbed the spiral steps of the tower –
up the steep steps of the bell cage, to the bourdon,
the great bumblebee, Emmanuel.
I stared at that bronze weight, the voice of Paris,
as if it was my father's voice
and I had climbed up his spine,
all thirteen tons of copper and tin,
the clapper half a ton of exorcised iron.
I washed the outside with holy oil for the sick,
the inside with chrism. Let all badness
be banished when he rings. Let the powers of the air
tremble – the hail and lightning
that fell from his tongue on our last days together.
I made the sign of the cross. His note
was F sharp, the hum
deep enough to reverberate through the rest of my life.
I stood upright in him.
I placed myrrh inside his mouth, incense
smoking like a last cigarette.
I praised him. I assembled the priests.
I mourned his death.
Storm clouds dispersed. Thunderbolts scattered.
I tolled in Sabbaths. I raised
my father's life to its hoists and rang him until I was deaf.
I proclaimed peace after bloodshed.

Acknowledgements

Many thanks to the editors of the following, in which some of these poems first appeared, sometimes in previous versions: *The Best British Poetry 2012* (Salt Publishing, editors Sasha Dugdale and Roddy Lumsden), *The Best British Poetry 2013* (Salt Publishing, editors Ahren Warner and Roddy Lumsden), *Connotation Press: An Online Artifact, The European English Messenger, Guernica, Magma, The Moth, Poem, Poetry, Poetry London, Poetry Review, Poetry Wales, Quadrant, The Rialto, The Stinging Fly*.

A portfolio of five of these poems won the 2013 Manchester Poetry Prize. Eight of these poems are included in *Fauverie*, a bilingual edition of my selected poems in China.

'Arrival of the Electric Eel', 'Black Jaguar at Twilight', 'Sleeping Black Jaguar', 'Blackbird', 'North China Leopard (Tao)', 'A Tray of Frozen Songbirds', 'Emmanuel', 'My Father's City' and 'Harpy Eagle Father' were recorded for The Poetry Archive in 2013, some with different titles. 'My Father's City' was recorded for the programme *Images as Strong as Sculptures: the Poetry of Pascale Petit*, broadcast in Poetica – ABC Radio National on 19 July 2014.

'Le Sang des Bêtes' was commissioned by Tom de Freston and was inspired by his painting *Hung*.

I am indebted to Les Murray for his continued support and for mentioning in a letter that François Mitterrand's last meal culminated in an ortolan. I am also indebted to Alain Gheerbrant for his detailed description of the Piaroa ant glove ritual in *The Impossible Adventure: Journey to the Far Amazon* (Victor Gollancz, 1953).

My thanks to the keepers and regular visitors of the Fauverie in the Ménagerie of the Jardin des Plantes, Paris, for their information, and especially to the residents for being themselves: Aramis the black jaguar, Karu the snow leopard, Leila and Tao the North China leopards, Samar the clouded leopard, and Black Ears the caracal. Aramis is now housed at the Parc Zoologique de Paris at Vincennes, in a larger enclosure.

I am grateful to Arts Council England for a Grant for the Arts in 2013. I am also grateful to the Society of Authors for an Authors' Foundation grant in 2011, and to the Royal Literary Fund for a Fellowship at the Courtauld Institute of Art in 2011-12. All of these enabled me to spend time in Paris to write this book.

Also by Pascale Petit

Heart of a Deer

The Zoo Father

The Huntress

The Treekeeper's Tale

What the Water Gave Me: Poems after Frida Kahlo

About the Author

Pascale Petit was born in Paris and grew up in France and in Wales. She has published six collections of poetry. Five poems from her latest book *Fauverie* won the 2013 Manchester Poetry Prize. Her fifth collection, *What the Water Gave Me: Poems after Frida Kahlo*, was shortlisted for both the TS Eliot Prize and the Wales Book of the Year and was Jackie Kay's Book of the Year in the *Observer*. Black Lawrence Press published an American edition in 2011. Three of Petit's collections have been shortlisted for the TS Eliot Prize and were featured as Books of the Year in the *Times Literary Supplement, Observer* and the *Independent*.

Her second collection *The Zoo Father* was a Poetry Book Society Recommendation, and was published in Mexico in a bilingual edition. A poem from it was shortlisted for a Forward Prize. Her selected poems are published in China. In 2004 the Poetry Book Society selected Petit as one of the Next Generation Poets and she has won numerous awards, including five from Arts Council England. Petit trained as a sculptor at the Royal College of Art and was a visual artist for the first part of her life. She is widely travelled, including in the Venezuelan Amazon, China and Nepal.

Visit the author's website and blog:
www.pascalepetit.co.uk
www.pascalepetit.blogspot.com

Well chosen words

Seren is an independent publisher with a wide-ranging list which includes poetry, fiction, biography, art, translation, criticism and history. Many of our books and authors have been on longlists or shortlists for - or won - major literary prizes, among them the Costa Award, the Man Booker, the Desmond Elliott Prize, The Writer's Guild Award, Forward Prize, and TS Eliot Prize.

At the heart of our list is a beautiful poem or a good story told well or an idea or history presented interestingly or provocatively. We're international in authorship and readership though our roots are here in Wales (Seren means Star in Welsh), where we prove that writers from a small country with an intricate culture have a worldwide relevance.

Our aim is to publish work of the highest literary and artistic merit that also succeeds commercially in a competitive, fast changing environment. You can help us achieve this goal by reading more of our books - available from all good bookshops and increasingly as e-books. You can also buy them at 20% discount from our website, and get monthly updates about forthcoming titles, readings, launches and other news about Seren and the authors we publish.